EDGE
BOOKS

DARING WILDFIRE RESCUES

by AMY WAESCHLE

Consultant:
Jackie White, Captain of Fire Investigations
and Homeland Security, Albuquerque Fire Department

CAPSTONE PRESS
a capstone imprint

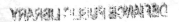

Edge Books are published by Capstone Press,
1710 Roe Crest Drive,
North Mankato, Minnesota 56003
www.mycapstone.com

Library of Congress Cataloging-in-Publication Data
Library of Congress Cataloging-in-Publication data is available on the Library of Congress website.
ISBN 978-1-5435-0112-4 (library binding)
ISBN 978-1-5435-0116-2 (paperback)
ISBN 978-1-5435-0120-9 (eBook pdf)

Editorial Credits
Editor: Lauren Dupuis-Perez
Book Designer: Sara Radka
Production Specialist: Katy LaVigne

Quote Sources
p.9, "Awful Splendour: A Fire History of Canada." UBC Press, 2007; p.12, "'We saw tornadoes of fire coming towards us': British-born grandfather tells of moment he led terrified family into the sea as Australian wildfires tore through their town." Daily Mail, Jan. 9, 2013; p.16, "1600 Yards to Freedom." Vertical Magazine, Sept. 30, 2014; p.22, "Victorian helicopter crewman gets bravery award for Black Saturday rescue." ABC, March 16, 2016; p.26, "Alcoa, Maryville Fire Departments help rescue 12 trapped by wildfire near Dollywood." The Daily Times, Dec. 2, 2016; p.29, "Man Rescued In Wildfire By Val And Amy Castor Shares Experience." News 9, April 6, 2016.

Image Credits
Getty Images: Brian Blanco, 25, Cameron Spencer, 11, Colin Anderson, Cover, David McNew, 27, Justin Sullivan, 15, Kip Evans/Design Pics, 7, Luis Ascui, 22, Mark Metcalfe, 12, Patrick Orton, 4, Quinn Rooney, 21, Steve Bly, 8; iStockphoto: BeyondImages, 13, ErinWilkins, Cover, 26, Givaga, 19, marekuliasz, 29, omersukrugoksu, 28, Squirescape, 10; Newscom: CB2/ZOB/Supplied by WENN.com, 23, Jason South/Fairfax Media via ZUMA Press, 20, Kukhmar Kirill/TASS via ZUMA Press, 18, Michael Pusnik Jr/US Navy/ZUMA Press, 16, Michael Routh/Ambient Images, 6, Randall Benton/Sacramento Bee/ZUMA Wire, 14, Ronen Tivony/NurPhoto via ZUMA Press, 17, Yin Bogu Xinhua News Agency, 24

Graphic elements by Book Buddy Media and Capstone Press.

Printed and bound in the USA.
010780S18

Table of Contents

Rescues in Wildfires

Many wildfires burn each year around the
world, but only a few become deadly disasters.

There hasn't been rain for weeks, and the air is hot and dry. On a faraway ridge, a thin column of smoke rises from the trees. Maybe it's from a campfire, or a small blaze from a lightning strike. A day later, the column has become a cloud of smoke. Soon many acres of forest are burning. The air becomes smoky. Ashes drift down like snow. It's a wildfire!

Fire needs fuel, oxygen, and a spark in order to burn. The fuel is wood or other burnable material. Oxygen comes from the air. The spark can be any heat source.

People cause most wildfires. The most common spark is from campfires that have not been put out completely. Fireworks, lightning, and cigarettes can also cause wildfires.

Just as dry firewood burns more easily than wet firewood, dry forests can **ignite** more easily. Forests that have experienced years of **drought** are more likely to burn. Dry weather and wind can make a fire more likely to spread. Wildfires burn almost 1 billion acres (0.4 billion hectares) of land worldwide every year.

ignite—to begin burning or to catch fire

drought—a long period of weather with little or no rainfall

Most fires burn slowly enough to allow people time to escape. Yet more than 330,000 people are killed by wildfires each year around the world. People usually get caught in wildfires when they wait too long to escape. Often, they try to escape at the last minute and find that they are trapped. They think their risk is low, but then conditions change due to wind or weather.

The victims of wildfires depend on firefighters and other rescuers for help. These brave rescuers risk their own lives to save the lives of others. Read on to uncover what it takes to jump into smoke and flames and make one of these daring rescues.

Firefighters work on crews of 2 to 20 people. They must be able to work well with others.

Large forest fires can grow quickly and burn for weeks or even months.

CHAPTER 1

Race to the Miramichi River

Almost 200 years ago, the Miramichi River was the
site of one of the deadliest fires in Canada's history.

In October 1825, the forests along the Miramichi River in New Brunswick, Canada, were dry. It was warm, and no rain had fallen for three months. On October 7, a fire broke out. It swept through the area like a hurricane.

In Newcastle, a family was overtaken by the flames. While his family ran to safety, the father stayed. He tried to gather important belongings. But the fire was soon upon him, and he had to run for his life.

The father raced to the Miramichi River. Hundreds of people were in the water to escape the flames. Bears, deer, raccoons, and cattle were also in the river. Some people tried to escape in boats, but many boats caught on fire. A group of people on one boat that didn't burn rescued the father and others in the river. The fire burned 5,000 square miles (8,000 square kilometers) and killed 160 people.

"The people of Newcastle had no idea of the fire being so near, the smoke having been so great all day that none could see where the flames were, until they came down upon them."

SURVIVOR
(NAME NOT RECORDED)

CHAPTER 2

A Watery Escape in Tasmania

Tasmania is an island state of Australia. It has a long history of bushfires.

In Tasmania, Australia, high temperatures of more than 105 degrees Fahrenheit (40 degrees Celsius) had caused a heat wave. The island was also experiencing a drought. Dozens of wildfires broke out in January 2013. Fueled by high winds, the fires exploded.

On January 4 in Dunalley, Tim and Tammy Holmes were taking care of their five grandchildren at their seaside home. The Holmeses knew there was a **bushfire** burning, but it was far away and moving in the opposite direction. They weren't worried. The morning was clear and it wasn't windy. However, the winds increased throughout the day and shifted. The fire changed course. By the afternoon, it was burning down the trees behind their house.

Fires in Tasmania in 2016 burned ancient trees that were 1,000 years old.

bushfire—fire in the countryside where the grass and bushes burn very fast; also the Australian word for wildfire

Wildfires can pollute the air for hundreds of miles. Breathing the smoke and ash can be very bad for people's health.

Tammy and the children raced to the end of their small dock. Tim stayed to protect the house. But the fire was all around him. He could barely see through the smoke. He gave up firefighting and hurried to the dock.

"We saw tornadoes of fire just coming across towards us and the next thing we knew everything was on fire, everywhere, all around us."

TIM HOLMES

The family escaped into the water. The hot, dry air was thick with smoke. The dock caught fire. Tim tried to put it out by scooping water with his hat, but it caught fire several more times. On shore, the fire consumed their house. They heard huge crashes, wood bursting into flames, and roofs and brick walls falling down. After several hours, Tim was able to pull their rowboat from the shore. Everyone jumped in. Tim pulled the boat into the raging wind along the shore to safety. After the fire, the only thing left of their house was the chimney.

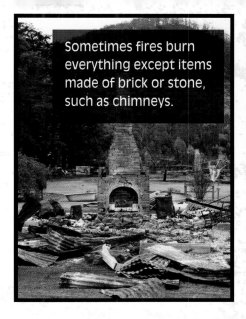

Sometimes fires burn everything except items made of brick or stone, such as chimneys.

How to Survive a Wildfire

The best way to stay safe in a fire is to follow **evacuation** warnings. Fire paths can change quickly. Call 911 with your location if you realize you are trapped.

- **If you are in a car**: Close the windows. Get on the floor and cover yourself. Use a coat, extra clothes, or a blanket. To keep from breathing smoke, keep your face close to the floor. Cover your mouth and nose with your arms or hands or a piece of clothing.

- **If you are on foot**: Find a clearing. Lie face down, cover yourself with a coat or extra clothing, and keep your mouth and nose close to the ground.

- **If you're in your home**: Close the windows and place wet towels or sheets at the base of all doors to keep smoke out. Stay away from the windows and the walls.

evacuation—the removal of large numbers of people in an area during a time of danger

CHAPTER 3

Helicopter Hero in California

Firefighters from across the United States were brought in to help fight the 2014 King Fire in California.

By September 15, 2014, a wildfire known as the King Fire had been burning out of control in California for two days. Helicopter pilot Gary Dahlen was at the scene, dropping water on the flames from a bucket that dangled below his helicopter.

On the ground, fire captain Kevin Fleming and his crew of 12 firefighters were digging ditches called fire lines. Fire lines interrupt a wall of flame and stop the fire from spreading. Downhill from the crew, a fire was **smoldering**. With the air so thick with smoke, Fleming didn't know they were in danger. By the middle of the day, shifting winds spread the fire up the slope. Suddenly, they were in the middle of a **crown fire**. Fleming radioed for help. Then he ordered his crew to take out their fire shelters. They climbed into their thin foil blankets and waited.

Firefighters routinely practice using their fire shelters.

smolder—to burn slowly without flames but usually with smoke

crown fire—a fire that spreads rapidly and jumps along the canopy of the forest trees

Helicopter pilots use bright orange Bambi Buckets to drop water right on target.

Gary Dahlen received the rescue call. He quickly flew his helicopter to the site. He saw the 12 silver shelters spread out on a dirt road. A wall of fire was racing toward them. Dahlen realized that the crew would not survive if they stayed.

Dahlen spotted a bare patch of ground 200 yards (180 meters) away. Using his radio, he told the crew to run. The firefighters sprinted through the smoke, their fire shelters flapping behind them like capes. Dahlen yelled to run faster. Finally, they reached the bare patch. The fire started to die down, and Fleming found an escape route. Dahlen picked them up and flew them to safety.

"At this point, I thought we were truly dead. The fire was all over the road above us, behind us, in front of us . . . It was like riding inside a wave on a surfboard. We were literally running through a tunnel of fire."

KEVIN FLEMING

Wildland Fire Rescue Workers

Dedicated crews of firefighters work hard each year to control wildfires. Here are some of the team members:

Firefighters: Firefighters work directly in or near fires. They dig fire lines with hand tools and chain saws. Some firefighters jump out of airplanes. Others are specially trained to fight fires in rugged and remote terrain.

Helicopter pilots: Helicopter pilots drop water on fires. From a nearby lake, they scoop water up in giant buckets that dangle from helicopters. They can also transport firefighters and their gear.

Fixed-wing aircraft pilots: The pilots of fixed-wing aircraft can drop large amounts of **fire retardant** or water. This slows down the fire so that ground crews can dig fire lines.

Heavy equipment operators: These workers use backhoes, bulldozers, and other heavy machines. The machines can create fire lines in steep terrain.

fire retardant—a chemical mix that firefighters spread from airplanes in order to keep a wildfire from spreading

CHAPTER 4

SOS in Siberia

Hot and dry conditions led to an intense fire season during the summer of 2012 in Siberia. Almost 2,000 wildfires burned 500,000 acres (200,000 ha) that year.

In August 2012, a couple and their son went berry-picking near Tomsk in Siberia, Russia. The area was experiencing the most severe wildfire season in 10 years. Temperatures had been high for months with no rainfall. This had made the **fuel load** extremely high. Many wildfires were burning. These fires would eventually burn an area the size of New Zealand. The air was full of thick smoke that mixed with **haze**.

The family became lost in the woods. The smoke had made it impossible to see. Fires closed in around them. Unable to escape, they realized they needed to signal for help. They chopped down birch trees. Birch trees have a white trunk, which can be seen from the air. In a clearing, they used the tree trunks to spell out "**SOS**." To survive, they ate berries and pine cones. After five days, a helicopter pilot noticed the signal. He was able to land and rescue the family.

The birch tree is the national tree of Russia.

fuel load—the amount of wood and dryness in a forest

haze—dust or mist that has filled the air so that you cannot see clearly

SOS—a signal sent out to call for urgent help

More than 5,000 firefighters helped fight the Black Saturday bushfires in 2009. This included pilots flying the Erickson Aircrane Helitanker.

Volunteers with the Country Fire Authority helped with clean-up efforts after the Black Saturday bushfire.

The Black Saturday bushfire was raging across the Australian countryside in August 2009. Police officer David Key was working with a helicopter crew helping with rescues. His station got a call from a news helicopter. The pilot had seen people trapped in a home with fire all around them. Key and his crew suited up and flew to the scene, where houses were exploding with flames.

The helicopter crew lowered Key to the ground. He hooked up a woman and her dog to be raised up to the helicopter. But the helicopter started to sink. There was too much smoke in the air and not enough oxygen. Without oxygen, helicopters can't fly.

Key unclipped the woman from the line. The helicopter just barely rose up over the trees. Once it regained its power, the pilot told them it was too dangerous. The only way out was to drive. The woman jumped into her vehicle. Key loaded up her horses. Two horses went into her trailer. The third horse was attached to a rope. The woman held the rope out the window and led the horse while she drove. Key drove in a separate car behind her. They just managed to escape as the flames closed in.

Once they made it through the flames, wild animals came alongside them on the road. Deer, kangaroos, and other animals appeared out of the forest. For a while, they were all moving together down the road and, finally, to safety. After the rescue, Key received a medal for his bravery.

> **"The house behind where we were was on fire and the fire was coming up on the righthand side. This was very, very close and very, very dangerous."**
>
> **DAVID KEY**

Most wild animals are able to escape wildfires by flying or running away, going underground, or going into bodies of water.

Volunteer groups and organizations such as the International Fund for Animal Welfare help wildlife that are injured or displaced by wildfires.

Rescuing Animals

Saving people is a rescuer's top priority, but what about livestock, pets, and other animals? Wildfire crews often rescue them too. They may load horses in trailers and drive them to safety. They may also set cows free from their pens so they can escape. Dogs and cats can ride in helicopters with their owners.

Sometimes firefighters even rescue wildlife. During the Black Saturday bushfire in Australia, firefighter Sam Tree noticed a koala sitting on the ground. It looked confused and had burned paws. Tree stopped his truck, got out, and gave the koala water. It drank and put a burned paw in Tree's hand. Tree took the koala to a shelter, where it was treated for its burns.

CHAPTER 6

Twelve Trapped in Tennessee

The 2016 Pigeon Forge fires killed 14 people and damaged almost 2,000 buildings.

Near Pigeon Forge, Tennessee, 12 people were staying in cabins during the week of Thanksgiving in 2016. Miles away, a wildfire started on November 23 in Great Smoky Mountains National Park. The fire burned slowly for several days. Fire officer Greg Salansky expected the **natural firebreaks** surrounding the fire to keep it from spreading.

But by November 28, the winds increased. **Spot fires** quickly spread the blaze to Pigeon Forge. The people staying in the cabins, including a father and his baby, tried to escape in their cars. The roads were blocked by fallen burning trees and downed power lines. One of the people used a cell phone to call for help. Behind them, cabins were bursting into flames. They were trapped.

natural firebreak—a river, body of water, or road that blocks a fire from spreading

spot fire—a new fire started by sparks or embers from a wildfire

Fire chief Darryl Kerley and his crew of five firefighters raced to the scene in their engine. Electric-company workers had to cut the power lines blocking their way. The fire crew arrived to find three cars stranded in the middle of the road. The firefighters could hear propane tanks exploding. Fire was all around them, and the flames were minutes away from consuming them all.

The people didn't want to leave their cars. They were terrified of the fire. Finally, the firefighters convinced the people to evacuate. The firefighters carried people's pets as the group hurried back downhill to the fire truck. They couldn't see. The smoke and flames were devouring the forest all around them. Finally, they reached the fire truck. The firefighters drove everyone to an evacuation shelter.

"I've been doing this for 21 years, and I've never seen it like this in my career—never. When we drove in there, and all this fire was on both sides of us."

KEVIN JAMES
FIREFIGHTER

Houses, cabins, and other buildings can burst into flames quickly once a wildfire reaches them.

Fire and Weather

Why are some fires easily **contained** while others rage out of control? Weather is a big reason. Hot, dry temperatures mixed with high winds is a recipe for disaster. Wind lifts burning material into the air. These "fire bombs" are carried miles away from the original fire and land in treetops. This starts new spot fires. This is also one way that houses catch fire. Burning material is carried by the wind and lands on a roof.

contain—to keep from spreading

CHAPTER 7

Farmer Survives Burnover

Local people who run heavy machinery for work are often called in during wildfires to help dig fire lines.

Storm chasing journalists Amy and Van Castor were tracking a wildfire on April 5, 2016. It was sweeping across Oklahoma farmland. They were driving along the edge of the flames when a wall of fire blew up in front of them.

Jason Perks was driving a road grader nearby. He was digging a fire line to protect a house across the street. Driven by high winds, the flames came closer. Perks tried to move his grader, but it became stuck in a ditch.

The Castors yelled to Perks to abandon the tractor. They moved their truck closer and yelled for him to jump in. Twelve-foot (3.7-m) flames began to swallow the tractor. Perks sprinted to the truck and dove inside. Van Castor reversed down the road, just as the flames began to rise over the truck's hood. The action was caught on camera, and the video received tens of thousands of views online.

> **"**I didn't realize it was that close. I knew it was close, but not that close.**"**
>
> **JASON PERKS**

Wildfire is unpredictable. It can change direction in an instant. In the right conditions, a manageable ground fire can explode into a wall of flames. When victims become trapped, rescuers spring into action. With bravery and determination, they do everything in their power to save lives.

Wildland Fire Danger Rating Systems

The chart outside many U.S. public lands shows the level of fire danger by color. Green is low and red is extreme. Australia also uses a color-based rating system. Other places, such as the United Kingdom, use a numbered scale. A small number means low risk and a large number means exceptional risk of fire. Experts studying fuel load and weather patterns work with a computer program to make a **forecast**. If fire danger is high, officials may **ban** campfires, fireworks, or the use of camp stoves.

storm chase—to track and physically follow extreme weather for fun, science, or news reporting

forecast—a report of future conditions

ban—to forbid or make something illegal

Glossary

ban (BAN)—to forbid or make something illegal

bushfire (BUSH-fyr)—fire in the countryside where the grass and bushes burn very fast; also the Australian word for wildfire

contain (kuhn-TAYN)—to keep from spreading

crown fire (KROWN FYR)—a fire that spreads rapidly and jumps along the canopy of the forest trees

drought (DROUT)—a long period of weather with little or no rainfall

evacuation (i-va-kyuh-WAY-shun)—the removal of large numbers of people in an area during a time of danger

fire retardant (FYR ree TAR-duhnt)—a chemical mix that firefighters spread from airplanes in order to keep a wildfire from spreading

forecast (FOR-kast)—a report of future conditions

fuel load (FYOOL LOHD)—the amount of wood and dryness in a forest

haze (HAYZ)—dust or mist that has filled the air so that you cannot see clearly

ignite (ig-NITE)—to begin burning or to catch fire

natural firebreak (NACH-ur-uhl FYR-brake)—a river, body of water, or road that blocks a fire from spreading

smolder (SMOHL-der)—to burn slowly without flames but usually with smoke

SOS (ES OH ES)—a signal sent out to call for urgent help

spot fire (SPOT FYR)—a new fire started by sparks or embers from a wildfire

storm chase (STORM CHAYS)—to track and physically follow extreme weather for fun, science, or news reporting

Read More

Curtis, Jennifer Keats. *Lucky Litter: Wolf Pups Rescued from Wildfire.* Mt. Pleasant, S.C.: Arbordale Publishing, 2015.

Garbe, Suzanne. *The Worst Wildfires of All Time.* Epic Disasters. North Mankato, Minn.: Capstone Press, 2013.

Thiessen, Mark. *Extreme Wildfire: Smoke Jumpers, High-Tech Gear, Survival Tactics, and the Extraordinary Science of Fire.* Washington, D.C.: National Geographic, 2016.

Internet Sites

Use FactHound to find Internet sites related to this book.

Visit *www.facthound.com*

Just type in 9781543501124 and go.

Check out projects, games and lots more at
www.capstonekids.com

Index